Salmon
COOKBOOK

Salmon COOKBOOK

PAULA AHLSÉN SÖDER

NEW HOLLAND

Contents

Foreword	5
About Salmon	6
Basic Recipes	10
Starters and Snacks	13
Lunches and Salads	57
Main Courses	101
Index	151

"Drink to others' health, but eat for your own."
Russian proverb

Salmon is a wonderful fish to cook and the results often exceed all expectations. Having once been an exclusive fish that was only served on special occasions, nowadays salmon is available for everyone to enjoy whenever they like. Sometimes we can all get stuck in a rut and end up making the same recipe over and over again, but there are endless ways to adapt salmon for you to explore.

Here I've chosen my own favourite recipes – try them and soon you'll start experimenting with tastes and combinations to find your own favourites. I always choose organic salmon and highly recommend that you choose the same if you possibly can as the taste is much better and the cost to the environment much less.

The recipes are arranged into appetizers, small dishes and snacks, lunches, salads and main courses, as well as basic recipes to help you get started. Even a simple salmon dish can seem unbelievably luxurious if you arrange it beautifully and serve it with a glass of good wine so vary your accompaniments to suit your mood and the occasion.

I hope this book will inspire you to have many fun moments in the kitchen together with the king of fish.

Paula Ahlsén Söder

About Salmon

Flavourful, adaptable and beautifully coloured, salmon has long been a favourite fish. Once seen as an exclusive party food, salmon is now much more affordable and can make a delicious everyday supper as well as an indulgent treat for dinner guests.

Farmed salmon has become widely available and now sits alongside wild salmon in our fishmongers and supermarkets. Farmed salmon often has an orange colour while wild salmon is significantly paler. The colour of the flesh depends on what the fish eats over the course of its life.

There is also organic farmed salmon. It comes from farms that take special care of the fish's living conditions and of the environment in and around the farm. For example, the fish food cannot contain any synthetic colours. For this reason, the colour of organic fish is more grey-rose.

Thanks to the fish's wonderful nutritional value, nutrition experts recommend that we eat fish for dinner or lunch 2–3 times a week.

The magnificent Atlantic salmon has a number of relatives. Rainbow trout and Arctic char are two of them. They can be used in the same way as Atlantic salmon in cooking. There is both wild and farmed rainbow trout; most of the char sold to shops and restaurants is farmed.

Farmed salmon is relatively high in fat, at about 20%. The fat of fish is soft and oily even at refrigerator temperature. The consistency of the fat makes oily fish like salmon and herring seem higher in fat than meat and cold cuts that actually have the same fat content. When you fry an unbreaded salmon steak, it releases a little fat and is therefore leaner after it's been fried, even if you use butter or oil in the frying pan.

The fat in fish is healthy. In salmon and other oily fish, there are omega-3 fatty acids, which are a special type of fat that has been shown to prevent heart and blood vessel disease, such as heart attacks and strokes. In recent years, there have even been studies that have shown that omega-3 fatty acids play an important role in the development of the brain in foetuses and young children. One portion of salmon (150 g) contains approximately four grams of omega-3. This is a good amount of healthy fatty acids; the recommended daily intake is 2–3 grams. Fish is also a good source of vitamin D and the important minerals selenium and iodine.

The oil in fish is delicate and can go off quickly, even in the freezer. When you buy a large portion of fresh salmon or if you go fishing yourself and want to keep some in the freezer, pack the fish tightly in plastic bags, mark them with the date and freeze them quickly. Oily fish has a storage life in the freezer of about three months.

Salmon that is going to be eaten more or less raw, for example if it is going to be raw-pickled or used in sushi or ceviche, should first be frozen for one day. This will kill any parasites in the fish.

The best temperature to keep fresh fish at is 2°C/35°F. Normal refrigerators have a temperature of between 4–8°C/39–46°F. Fish fillets that are in plastic bags will stay fresh for about 2 days in a refrigerator that is set to 8°C/46°F. Some refrigerators have a special cold zone for delicate items; fresh fish should be kept in there. The best way to tell if fish is fresh is to smell it. It should smell fresh and of the sea.

Salmon is a popular fish for anglers. The best season for fishing is during the summer and autumn. Salmon is a migratory fish that, oddly enough, can live in fresh, salt or brackish water. Farmed fish has no seasons and is just as good all year round.

Basic Recipes

GRAVLAX

In times past, raw-pickling was a way of preserving fish when salt was very expensive. To raw-pickle the fish, you had to place fir twigs and bark in a pit dug into the ground. The lightly salted fish would be put into the pit and covered with more sticks and earth. Gravlax takes its name from this process: in Swedish, 'grav' means grave or pit while 'lax' means salmon. Today people continue to raw-pickle salmon to get that special taste and consistency.

To make your own gravlax, choose a fillet from the middle of a large salmon for a more even result. Scrape and dry the salmon, but don't rinse it.

PER KILO OF SALMON:

50 g (2 oz) sugar
50 g (2 oz) salt
10 white peppercorns, crushed
300 g (10 oz) dill, coarsely chopped
(alternatively, season with orange, ginger, rosemary, or pink peppercorns)

Slice the salmon along the backbone. Remove the backbone and carefully remove all the small bones using tweezers. Stir the sugar and salt together and rub the mixture into the fish. Spread about a third of the dill in the bottom of a shallow dish. Place one of the salmon halves skin-side down on top of the dill. Sprinkle with more dill and pepper.

Place the other salmon half on top with the skin-side up. Cover the salmon with the remaining dill and place foil over the top. Leave the fish somewhere cold and dark for 2 days. Turn it a few times during that period. If the salmon is not going to be eaten immediately, it is fine to freeze it.

CURED SALMON

If a fish is cured, that means it is lightly salted. Most fish can be cured and the result is a fillet with a somewhat firmer consistency. Fish can be quickly cured in a couple of hours to add flavour and firm texture but to preserve it, it needs a couple of days.

PER KILO OF SALMON:

50 g (2 oz) sugar
100 g (3 ½ oz) salt
10 white peppercorns, crushed
300–400 g (10–14 oz) dill, chopped

Slice the salmon along the backbone. Remove the backbone and carefully remove all the small bones. Place the salmon halves skin-side down in a dish. Mix the sugar, salt and white pepper together and rub the mixture into the fish. Sprinkle with the dill. Cover the fish and leave it in the refrigerator for two days. Turn it a few times to make sure the fish is evenly cured.

WARM-SMOKED SALMON

Warm-smoking fish is an old preserving and flavouring method. The smoking takes place in a smoker at a temperature between 60–120°C/140–248°F for 30–40 minutes, depending on the size of the fish.

COLD-SMOKED SALMON

The smoking takes place in the same way as for warm-smoked fish, except at a significantly lower temperature, around 30°C/70°F, and for a longer period of time, around 5 hours.

COOKED IN THE OVEN

The best way to get perfect results in the oven is to get a digital meat thermometer. Place the thermometer in the thickest part of the salmon and set the timer to the desired temperature. Remember that when the salmon is taken out of the oven, its temperature will rise a couple of degrees.

TEMPERATURES:

Salmon fillet: around 48°C/110°F
Whole salmon: around 52°C/125°F

Slow cooking at 100–125°C/225–240°F is a very gentle way of cooking and the result is an evenly cooked and juicy fish.

Quickly cooking salmon in the oven at 175–225°C/325–425°F can be a little more uneven, because the edges cook first, but it is much faster.

POACHED IN A SAUCEPAN

Salmon should never be boiled, just simmered. Here is how you make a good poaching liquid:

PER LITRE OF WATTER:

1–1½ tbsp salt
3–4 white peppercorns
a few bay leaves

If you want, you can add a little vinegar or vinegar essence. This will make the fish turn a paler colour. Even when you poach, it can be useful to use a thermometer.

APPROXIMATE COOKING TIMES:

3 cm (1 in) thick fish: 5 minutes
6 cm (2 in) thick fish: 10 minutes

TO FRY SALMON

Always pat fish dry with kitchen paper before frying. The frying pan should be hot when you add the fish, but lower the temperature as soon as the salmon has been placed in the pan. Fry the salmon in butter or oil or make a mixture of both. Fry the salmon fillet for 2–3 minutes on each side.

SALMON IN FOIL

Wrapping salmon in foil is an ideal way to cook it as you can add whatever seasonings you like and you'll be sure that all the flavours will stay in the package.

TEMPERATURES AND COOKING TIMES:

Oven temperature: 200°C/400°F/gas mark 6
Whole fish: 25 minutes
Fillet: 15 minutes

TO BARBECUE OR GRILL:

Make sure the temperature is really hot before you put salmon on the barbecue or under the grill. On a barbecue, the charcoal should be really hot, grey all over, and with no flames. The grill rack should be about 30 cm from the embers or grill so the fish doesn't get burned. Let the grill rack get warm before the salmon is placed on it. To help stop the fish from sticking, brush both the fish and the grill with oil. Use a grill basket or a broiler to make grilling even easier.

COOKING TIMES:

Salmon in foil: 15 minutes
Smaller fillets or skewer: 2–3 minutes on each side.
Large fillet: 10 minutes. Keep the skin on the salmon so the fish doesn't fall apart and grill the skin-side last.

Starters and Snacks

Fantastic starters help to build expectations for the main course and salmon is the perfect beginning to a meal with friends and family.

toasted open salmon sandwich with gravlax sauce

INGREDIENTS

4 slices wholemeal bread
2 tbsp butter
4 small lettuce leaves
2 hard-boiled eggs, sliced
4 slices gravlax (about 150 g/5 oz)
slices of lemon, to garnish

GRAVLAX SAUCE:
3½ tbsp sweet mustard
2 tsp Dijon mustard
1 tbsp sugar
1 tbsp white wine vinegar
100 ml (3½ fl oz) rapeseed oil
3½ tbsp finely chopped dill
salt and freshly ground black pepper

SERVES 4, COOKING TIME 25 MINUTES

An easy-to-make, classic toasted sandwich is just as good as an appetizer or as a late evening meal. You can toast the bread in a toaster, but bread fried in butter makes the sandwich even better.

Remove the crusts from the slices of bread and fry the slices lightly in butter on both sides. Place the slices of toast on a serving dish or on four small dishes.

Place a lettuce leaf on each slice of bread, then 2–3 slices of egg and one slice of salmon. Drizzle the gravlax sauce on top. Garnish with slices of lemon and sprigs of dill.

Gravlax sauce:
Mix together the mustards, sugar and white wine vinegar. Season with salt and pepper. Carefully add the oil a little at a time and whisk well until the sauce turns creamy. Add the dill and mix again. You can make the gravlax sauce a day in advance.

salmon tartare

INGREDIENTS

500 g (1 lb 2 oz) gravlax
3–4 pickled cucumbers, chopped
2 red onions, finely chopped
6 hard-boiled eggs, chopped
2 ripe avocados, sliced and with
 the stone removed
4–6 raw egg yolks in halves of
 eggshells
4 tbsp large capers
1–2 lemons
1 jar lumpfish caviar (80 g/3 oz),
 red or black, or whitefish caviar
freshly ground black pepper

Tip!

It is easier if you cut the
salmon into pieces with scissors instead of slicing it with
a knife.

SERVES 4, COOKING TIME 25 MINUTES

The name tartare is used for dishes that contain finely
chopped raw fish or meat with various accompaniments.
Here I serve the finely cut salmon on a large dish with all
the seasonings and accompaniments around it. It looks
beautiful and everyone can choose the ingredients they like
best.

Slice the salmon into small cubes and place in a pile in the
middle of a large dish, preferably a slightly deep one. Make
little piles of the pickled cucumbers, onion, egg, capers and
avocado around the salmon. Squeeze a little lemon juice over
the avocado so it doesn't turn brown. Place the egg yolks in
their shells around the dish.

Slice the lemon and place the wedges around the edges of
the plate. Put out dollops of caviar. Season with pepper and, if
desired, chopped dill.

cured salmon with grapefruit

SERVES 4, COOKING TIME 20 MINUTES

The saltiness of salmon together with the fruitiness of the grapefruit, the spice of the jalapeño and the mild avocado makes this dish irresistible. It looks even more beautiful when you add some little red cherry tomatoes as decoration.

Drape the salmon slices on a plate. Peel the grapefruit and slice away all the white pith. Slice small pieces of the fruit and distribute them over the salmon. Save any extra grapefruit juice. Scatter the jalapeño and spring onions over the plate.

Place the avocado slices on top of the salmon. Pour all the grapefruit juice on top. If you don't have much, use the juice from the other half of the grapefruit. Garnish with cherry tomatoes and sprinkle some black pepper over everything.

INGREDIENTS

300 g (10½ oz) salted salmon in
  slices, or cold-smoked salmon
½–1 red grapefruit
6–8 mild jalapeño peppers,
  chopped
2–3 spring onions, chopped
2 avocados, sliced
6–8 cherry tomatoes
freshly ground black pepper

sushi with salmon and lemon

INGREDIENTS

200 g (7 oz) salmon fillet
2 lemons, sliced, plus a little
 lemon juice
100 ml (3½ fl oz) soya sauce
2 tsp wasabi
fresh coriander, to serve

Tip!

**You can also dip the lemon
slices in the wasabi soy.**

SERVES 4, COOKING TIME 15 MINUTES, PLUS CHILLING TIME

This is fast sushi for those who don't have a lot of time. The lemon slices quickly and simply marinate the salmon in a few hours in the refrigerator. It is important that the salmon has been frozen when it is to be eaten raw.

Slice the salmon into small oblong pieces. Thread lemon slices and salmon alternately onto wooden skewers. Squeeze a little lemon juice over the skewers and place them in the refrigerator for a few hours.

Divide the soya sauce amongst 4 small bowls and put a little wasabi in each.

Serve the skewers with a bowl of soya sauce to dip them in, some fresh coriander and perhaps a little rice.

salmon bruschetta

SERVES 4, COOKING TIME 30 MINUTES

Bruschetta is often served as an appetizer or snack in Italy and is composed of grilled bread that has been rubbed with garlic and olive oil. It can be eaten as it is but often it is topped with chopped tomatoes. Here I've made it slightly more filling by serving it with a slice of salmon.

Preheat the oven to 200°C/400°F/gas mark 6. Slice the baguette down the middle and then halve the pieces. Mince 2 garlic cloves and sprinkle over the bread, then brush with 2 tbsp olive oil. Bake the bread in the oven for a couple of minutes.

Mix the chilli flakes, 1 chopped garlic clove, tomatoes and spring onions together and fry everything in a little olive oil for a few minutes. Season with salt, a pinch of sugar and black pepper.

Spread the mixture over the bread and place a slice of salmon over each piece. Squeeze over the lime juice and garnish with fresh coriander.

INGREDIENSER

1 baguette
3 garlic cloves
3 tbsp olive oil
½ tsp chilli flakes
4 large tomatoes, finely chopped
4 spring onions, finely sliced
200 g (7 oz) smoked salmon in slices
juice of 1 lime
pinch of sugar
salt and freshly ground black pepper
fresh coriander, to garnish

salmon rolls with cream cheese and wasabi

INGREDIENTS

125 g (4½ oz) cream cheese
1 tsp wasabi
1 tsp dried herbs
4 slices gravlax or cold-smoked
   salmon, about 200 g (7 oz)

TO SERVE:
Different types of lettuce, cherry
tomatoes, sugar snap peas, roasted
seeds, such as pumpkin or sunflower seeds

SERVES 4, COOKING TIME 20 MINUTES

Cream cheese and wasabi are a perfect combination in this salmon roll that packs a punch. Wasabi is like horseradish, which you could use as an alternative if you can't get wasabi. If you serve it with vegetables, these rolls are a complete light meal.

Mix the cheese with the wasabi and herbs. Taste it to check the heat of the wasabi. Spread the mixture on the slices of salmon and roll them up. The salmon slices shouldn't be too thin as this makes them difficult to roll.

Serve them with lettuce leaves, tomatoes and sugar snap peas. Sprinkle with roasted seeds.

salmon salsa with coriander

INGREDIENTS

2 tomatoes, chopped
1 avocado, chopped
1 red onion, chopped
1 medium chilli, deseeded and
  chopped, or ½ tsp chilli flakes
1 garlic clove, crushed
juice of 1 lime
1 bunch fresh coriander, chopped
1 tbsp olive oil
400 g (14 oz) gravlax
salt and freshly ground black
  pepper

SERVES 4, COOKING TIME 25 MINUTES, PLUS CHILLING TIME

This traditional salsa works really well with gravlax. It's perfectly spicy and sour and is perfect as a light meal on its own or as a zingy side dish.

Mix the chopped tomatoes, avocado and onion with the crushed garlic and chilli. Squeeze the juice from the limes and add it to the mixture. Add the coriander and the olive oil. Season with salt and pepper.

Divide the salsa amongst small plates and put it in the refrigerator until ready to serve. Slice the gravlax into small pieces and place on top of the salsa.

salmon cups with feta and avocado crème

SERVES 4. COOKING TIME 10 MINUTES

In this recipe, feta cheese is accompanied by avocado. These flavours, combined with gravlax, make a stylish dish with a mild flavour. I've added a little grapefruit to the salad for acidity.

Mix the feta cheese, mashed avocado and crème fraîche in a bowl. Squeeze in the lemon juice and season with salt and black pepper. Mix well to form a smooth mixture.

Lay out the salmon slices and spread with the mixture; the slices shouldn't be too thin. Roll the slices so they form a cup shape with the filling inside. Top each cup with a dollop of caviar.

INGREDIENTS

200 g (7 oz) gravlax, about 4 slices
125 g (4 ½ oz) feta cheese
1 avocado, mashed
1-2 tbsp crème fraîche
juice of half a lemon
salt and black pepper
1 x 80-g (3-oz) jar red or black
  lumpfish caviar
Serve with: lettuce, tomatoes,
  pea shoots, half a grapefruit,
  lemon and dill

Tips!

Place the lettuce on a serving tray and put the cups on top. Decorate the tray with tomatoes, pea shoots, lemon and dill and scatter over slices of grapefruit.

blinis with salmon and caviar

INGREDIENTS

300 ml (10½ fl oz) milk
1 sachet easy-blend yeast
50 g (2 oz) plain flour
100 g (3½ oz) buckwheat flour
2 eggs, separated
50 g (2 oz) butter, plus extra for
  frying

150 g (5½ oz) whitefish caviar
4 tbsp finely chopped cold-smoked
  salmon (about 150 g/5½ oz)
1 red onion, finely chopped
200 ml (7 fl oz) crème fraîche or
  smetana
dill and lemon slices, to garnish

SERVES 4, COOKING TIME 1 HOUR

This is a luxurious classic dish that can still compete with newer recipes. Crispy blinis, lightly sour from the yeast and buckwheat together with salmon and caviar make up one of the tastiest dishes I know, especially when paired with a glass of Champagne.

Warm the milk to body temperature, be careful to not overheat. Pour the yeast into a mixing bowl and pour the milk over it. Add both the flours and whisk until smooth. Add the egg yolks to the mixture along with a pinch of salt. Leave the batter to rise at room temperature for about 30 minutes.

Melt the butter and set aside to cool. Whisk the egg whites until firm and mix them and the melted butter in a bowl gently. Melt a knob of butter in a frying pan. Pour in some batter to make a pancake of about 12 cm (5 in) in diameter. Brown the blinis over a medium heat, turning so they are beautifully golden brown on both sides.

Place the blinis on small plates as soon as they are ready. Add some caviar, salmon and onion on top and finish with a large heap of crème fraîche or smetana. Decorate with dill and lemon slices.

salmon hors d'oeuvre

SERVES 4, COOKING TIME 10 MINUTES, PLUS CHILLING TIME

This recipe is almost too simple, but it's fantastic and why should you make things unnecessarily difficult?

Peel the watermelon and cut it into 2 cm cubes (nowadays the seeds are so small that you don't have to remove them all). Cut the feta into cubes of the same size. Cut the kiwis or apricots and cut them into cubes and cut the salmon into pieces. Thread the feta, melon, kiwi/apricot and salmon onto cocktail sticks.

Mix together all the ingredients for the marinade and brush it over the salmon hors d'oeuvres. Place them in the refrigerator for a couple of hours before serving.

Decorate with mint leaves.

INGREDIENTS

300 g (10½ oz) watermelon
100 g (3½ oz) feta cheese
4 kiwis or apricots
100 g (3½ oz) gravlax, in pieces
cocktail sticks

MARINADE:
2 tbsp chopped mint
1–2 tbsp liquid honey
juice of 1 lime
1 tbsp olive oil
mint leaves, to garnish

salmon skewers with parsley and melon

INGREDIENTS

about 200 g (7 oz) gravlax in
  pieces
melon, such as honeydew
1 pinch chilli flakes
50 g (2 oz) fresh parsley, chopped

LIME SAUCE:
1 lime
200 ml (7 fl oz) Greek yogurt
100 g (3½ oz) lemon balm,
  chopped
2 tsp runny honey
freshly ground black pepper

Tips!

**You can also add large prawns,
which look and taste fantastic.**

SERVES 4, COOKING TIME 20 MINUTES

**Spicy and mild in a perfect combination, together with the
cooling powers of honeydew.**

Slice the salmon and melon into equally sized cubes and
thread them onto wooden skewers. Mix the chilli flakes and
parsley and roll the skewers in the mixture.

Grate the peel of the washed lime and squeeze the juice into
a bowl. Add the yogurt and lemon balm. Mix into a sauce. Season
with honey and black pepper.

salmon salad
with dill and lime

INGREDIENTS

200 g (7 oz) cold-smoked salmon
  in slices
2 bunches fresh dill, chopped
2 hard-boiled eggs, chopped
1 red onion, chopped
300–400 ml (10–14 fl oz) sour
  cream
1 x 80 g (3 oz) jar capelin caviar or
  lumpfish caviar
chilli flakes
salt and freshly ground black
  pepper

SERVES 4, COOKING TIME 20 MINUTES

This makes a great festive starter or a beautiful 'cocktail' on a buffet. Anyone would be happy to have a glass of this in their hand. To make it even more special, use whitefish caviar rather than lumpfish.

Chop the salmon into small pieces but save two slices. Place the salmon pieces in a mixing bowl and add most of the chopped dill, reserving a little for garnish. Add the chopped eggs and onion then the sour cream and caviar. Squeeze the lime juice into the mixture and season with chilli flakes, salt and freshly ground black pepper.

Divide the mixture between beautiful glasses to serve. Shred the remaining salmon slices and place them on top. Add a little more dill to garnish and place a slice of lime on the side of each glass.

open sandwich with poached salmon

INGREDIENTS

4 large slices of bread
butter, for spreading
8 cold boiled new potatoes, sliced
4 hard-boiled eggs, sliced
about 200 g (7 oz) cold poached
   salmon, see p. 71
4–8 tbsp hollandaise sauce, see
   p. 71
1 bunch fresh dill, coarsely
   chopped
salt and freshly ground black
   pepper

SERVES 4, COOKING TIME 15 MINUTES

A perfect sandwich if you have leftover poached salmon. To make a stronger tasting sandwich, replace the butter with caviar. If you don't have any leftover hollandaise, use mayonnaise instead.

Spread butter on the bread. Place the sliced potato and egg on top and season with salt and pepper. Add the salmon pieces and drizzle a few tablespoons of sauce over them. Sprinkle with dill and season with salt and pepper.

salmon pinwheels

SERVES 4, COOKING TIME 45 MINUTES

Crispy treats that melt in your mouth. You can make these in advance and warm them in the oven for 2–3 minutes before the guests arrive.

Preheat the oven to 200°C/400°F/gas mark 6. Line a baking sheet with greaseproof paper.

Roll out the pastry sheets to double their size. Squeeze out the spinach to remove as much water as you can. Spread the spinach over the pastry and season with black pepper and nutmeg. Put the salmon slices on top and roll up the pastry. Turn the pastry so the fold is underneath. Slice the rolls into pieces about 2 cm thick with a sharp knife. Place them on the baking tray and bake in the oven until the puff pastry is crispy, about 15 minutes. Watch carefully so they don't burn. When they come out of the oven, sprinkle with sea salt and chopped dill.

INGREDIENTS

2 sheets ready-rolled puff pastry sheets, defrosted
200 g (7 oz) spinach, defrosted if frozen
1 tsp nutmeg
4 slices gravlax (about 100 g/3 ½ oz)
salt and freshly ground black pepper
chopped dill, to garnish

canapés with salmon and caviar

INGREDIENTS

4 slices of white bread
2 tbsp butter
4 tbsp red onion, finely chopped
4 tbsp cold-smoked salmon, finely
  chopped
4 tbsp whitefish caviar
1 lemon
freshly ground black pepper

Tip!

If you want, you can use lumpfish caviar instead of whitefish caviar and then you can add a little sour cream.

SERVES 4, COOKING TIME 10 MINUTES

A wonderful pre-dinner snack with my favourites – salmon and whitefish caviar!

Remove the crusts from the bread and spread lightly with butter. Put the chopped onion on top. Place the salmon on one half and whitefish caviar on the other.

Put a wedge of lemon on a toothpick and stick one in the middle of every canapé. Grind a little black pepper on top.

salmon pâté
with sardine sauce

INGREDIENTS

loaf tin that holds about 1.5 litres
  (2½ pints)
butter, for greasing
500 g (1 lb 2 oz) salmon fillet with
  the skin removed
75 g (2½ oz) cold-smoked salmon
1 tsp salt
2 eggs
400 ml (13 fl oz) double cream
1 red chilli, finely chopped
3 tbsp finely chopped dill
1 lemon, juice
500 g (1 lb 2 oz) prawns
lemon slices, to garnish

SARDINE SAUCE:
5–6 sardine fillets, chopped
300 ml (10½ oz) sour cream
1–2 tbsp capers
1 tbsp mayonnaise
juice of ½ lemon
freshly ground black pepper

SERVES 4, COOKING TIME 1 HOUR 30 MINUTES

This pâté is not at all difficult to make, despite the long list of ingredients and instructions, so don't be put off!

Preheat the oven to 180°C/350°F/gas mark 4. Grease the loaf tin.

Chop all the salmon into pieces, place in a food processer and blend. Add a little salt, the eggs and the cream and mix again. Add the chilli, dill and lemon juice. Pour half of the mixture into the loaf tin.

Peel and chop the prawns and place most of them on top of the mixture, saving a few for decoration. Pour the rest of the mixture on top and carefully shake the tin so the surface is even. Cover with foil. Place the tin in a large roasting dish and fill the dish with water to half-way up the loaf tin. Put the whole thing in the oven and bake for about an hour. Take out the tin when the pâté is firm, then let it cool.

Turn out the pâté onto a beautiful serving dish and leave it for an hour to cool completely. Garnish with prawns and lemon slices and serve with the sardine sauce.

Sardine Sauce:
Mix the sardines with the sour cream, capers and mayonnaise. Squeeze the lemon juice into the sauce and season with black pepper. Mix well and pour into a bowl.

smoked salmon with goats' cheese pesto

SERVES 4, COOKING TIME 20 MINUTES

I used to make this dish with air-dried ham and just basil in the pesto, but I've since tried lots of variations on the recipe. Try it with different types of soft cheeses and add in various seeds, such as pumpkin, sesame and sunflower seeds.

Roast the pine nuts in a dry frying pan until they have coloured slightly. Watch them very carefully as they will burn easily. Place the pine nuts, goats' cheese, basil and lettuce in a food processor. Add the oil and lemon juice and mix until smooth. Add the garlic and a little black pepper then mix again.

Place the salmon slices on a large serving dish and spoon the pesto into the middle. Garnish with pine nuts, olives, red onion and herbs.

INGREDIENTS

125 g (4½ oz) pine nuts
125 g (4½ oz) goats' cheese
50 g (2 oz) fresh basil
75 g (2½ oz) lettuce
2 tbsp olive oil
2 tbsp lemon juice
1–2 garlic cloves, minced
300 g (10½ oz) cold-smoked
   salmon in thin slices
freshly ground black pepper

TO GARNISH:
roasted pine nuts
olives of various colours
finely chopped red onion
mixed herbs

salmon rolls with prawn filling

SERVES 4, COOKING TIME 15 MINUTES

INGREDIENTS

200 ml (7 fl oz) crème fraîche
1 red onion, finely chopped
1 x 80 g (3 oz) jar lumpfish caviar
2 tbsp finely chopped dill
200 g (7 oz) coarsely chopped
  prawns
juice of 1 lime
½–1 tsp cayenne pepper or chilli
  flakes
freshly ground black pepper
8 slices smoked salmon, not too
  thin (about 300 g/10½ oz)

TO GARNISH:
seeds and nuts
rocket
baby lettuce leaves

Here I fill cold-smoked salmon with a variation on the traditional Scandinavian Skagen salad, but with a little more bite in it from the cayenne pepper or chilli flakes.

Mix the crème fraîche, red onion, caviar, dill and prawns together. Season with a little of the lime juice, cayenne pepper or chilli flakes and black pepper.

Spread the salmon out and separate into slices. Spoon a little of the crème fraîche mixture onto each slice and roll up. If necessary, use a toothpick to hold each roll together.

Roast seeds, such as sunflower or pumpkin seeds, in a hot, dry frying pan. Watch them carefully so they don't burn. On small plates, make a bed of rocket and baby lettuce and place the salmon rolls on top. Sprinkle with plenty of the roasted seeds as well as dill, rings of red onion and lemon wedges.

salmon parcels with melon and mussels

SERVES 4, COOKING TIME 15 MINUTES

This is a perfect accompaniment to drinks and is lovely and easy to make. Serve it with a dry white wine or just sparkling water with lots of lemon slices and mint leaves.

Slice the melon into cubes. Divide each salmon slice into 4 parts. Roll half the salmon slices around the pieces of melon and half around the mussels. Stick the cocktail sticks through them.

Serve them on different dishes so guests can choose what they like.

INGREDIENTS

250 g (9 oz) melon, such as honeydew or musk melon
6 slices smoked salmon or gravlax
  (about 300 g/10½ oz)
12 large cooked mussels
cocktail sticks

salmon balls with dill

INGREDIENTS

200 g (7 oz) cold-smoked salmon
  or gravlax, finely chopped
a little olive oil
100 g (3½ oz) dill, coarsely
  chopped
juice of 1 lime

SERVES 4, COOKING TIME 20 MINUTES

Serve these salmon balls on individual spoons so guests can handle them more easily. They can be made several hours in advance and kept in the refrigerator.

Roll the salmon pieces into small balls, like meatballs. Brush all over each one with olive oil and roll them in the chopped dill. Place the salmon balls on a serving dish and squeeze over a little lime juice.

salmon ceviche

INGREDIENTS

200 g (7 oz) salmon fillet
juice of 2 limes
1–2 tbsp olive oil
1 avocado
1 kiwi, peeled and sliced
2 tomatoes, chopped
1 tbsp chopped coriander
1 spring onion, finely sliced
1 red chilli, deseeded and finely
  chopped
salt and freshly ground black
  pepper

SERVES 4, COOKING TIME 30 MINUTES, PLUS CHILLING TIME

Ceviche is a fish dish from South America that is comprised of raw fish that has been marinated in citrus, such as lime juice. You season it with chilli and perhaps some sweet fruit. It's typical to use white fish for ceviche but salmon works really well. Since the fish isn't cooked, it ought to have been frozen first to kill any parasites.

Cut the salmon into small cubes and place them in a bowl. Squeeze over the lime juice and pour olive oil on top. Season with salt and pepper. Cover the bowl and leave the fish to marinate in the refrigerator for 4–5 hours. Stir now and again.

Peel the avocado and remove the stone, then cut the flesh into small pieces and place them in a bowl. Add the kiwi and chopped tomatoes to the bowl, then add the coriander and spring onion. Add the chilli and give everything a good mix.

Carefully remove the salmon pieces from the marinade and mix them into the salsa. Pour a little of the marinade on top.

Serve in a cocktail glass.

Lunches and Salads

With delicious salads, pies and soups, lunch can be a wonderful mealtime
— especially if brought somewhere in a picnic basket to enjoy outdoors.

salmon carpaccio
with dill oil

INGREDIENTS

500 g (1 lb 2 oz) gravlax, thinly
   sliced
200 g (7 oz) mixed seeds, such
   as pine nuts, sunflower seeds or
   pumpkin seeds
Parmesan shavings

DILL OIL:
100 g (3½ oz) dill, chopped
100 ml (3½ fl oz) rapeseed oil
salt and freshly ground black
   pepper

SERVES 4, COOKING TIME 25 MINUTES

A classic carpaccio uses thin slices of raw beef but this variation with salmon is a real treat. In Italy, they drizzle olive oil on top and sprinkle with pine nuts and basil. Here the pine nuts remain but the basil has been replaced with dill oil.

Begin with the dill oil. Blend the dill and rapeseed oil in a food processor until smooth. Season with salt and black pepper.

Roast the seed mixture in a dry frying pan. Watch the seeds very carefully as they will burn quickly.

Place the slices of salmon on a serving plate and scatter over the roasted seeds. Add the Parmesan shavings and drizzle with the dill oil. Garnish with chopped dill.

salmon wraps

SERVES 4, COOKING TIME 20 MINUTES

These wraps are perfect for eating outdoors as they can be deliciously messy!

Slice the salmon into pieces. Remove the stones from the avocados and cut the flesh into slices. Peel, deseed and slice the melon into long, thin pieces.

Divide the salmon, lettuce, avocado and melon between the tortillas. Sprinkle with the onions. Add a spoonful of yogurt, some coriander and drizzle everything with lime juice. Season with fennel seeds, salt and black pepper.

Fold in the edges and roll the tortillas up.

INGREDIENTS

600 g (1 lb 6 oz) cold-smoked
    salmon in pieces
2 avocados
1 small melon, such as a canta-
    loupe
1 romaine lettuce
8 small flour tortillas
2 onions, sliced and roasted
200 ml (7 fl oz) Greek yogurt
1 bunch fresh coriander
juice of 1 lime
1 tsp fennel seeds
salt and freshly ground black
    pepper

salmon salad with fruit and mozzarella

INGREDIENTS

100 g (3½ oz) sunflower seeds
200 g (7 oz) mixed lettuce leaves
150 g (5 oz) mozzarella
½ melon, such as cantaloupe
2 avocados
2 peaches or nectarines
8–10 cherry tomatoes in various
   colours
500–600 g (1 lb 4 oz–1 lb 6 oz)
   cold-smoked salmon, thinly
   sliced
2 limes
salt and freshly ground black
   pepper
basil leaves, to garnish

SERVES 4, COOKING TIME 20 MINUTES

Fresh fruit and smoked salmon are amazing together. Choose whatever fruit is in season for the freshest taste.

Roast the sunflower seeds in a dry, hot frying pan. Watch them carefully and stir often because they roast quickly. Arrange the lettuce on a large, slightly deep plate. Deseed the melon and remove the stones from the avocados and peaches. Slice the mozzarella, melon, avocados and peaches and distribute them beautifully over the dish. Halve the tomatoes and add them to the plate. Separate the salmon slices into smaller pieces and set them out in small rose shapes around the plate.

Sprinkle with the sunflower seeds and squeeze over some lime juice. Season with salt and freshly ground black pepper.

salmon salad with new potatoes

Serves 4, cooking time 1 hour

This is a really summery salad that is just as good on a midsummer buffet as for a simple lunch.

Boil the potatoes until soft then set aside and leave to cool. Cut the potatoes into cubes and place them in a bowl. Mix the onions, olives and capers with the potatoes.

Make a sauce with the yogurt, mustard and fresh herbs. Pour the yogurt sauce over the potato salad and mix well. Season with sea salt and black pepper.

Cut the salmon into small cubes and place them on top of the potato salad. Sprinkle with more olives and capers. Serve with freshly baked bread.

INGREDIENTS

1 kg (2 lb 4 oz) new potatoes
2–3 spring onions, chopped
200 g (7 oz) pitted green olives
50 g (2 oz) capers
300 ml (10½ oz) Greek yogurt
2 tbsp Dijon mustard
100 g (3½ oz) chopped fresh
  herbs, such as parsley, basil,
  mint, lemon balm, oregano
salt and freshly ground black
  pepper
400 g (14 oz) gravlax in pieces
olives and capers, to garnish

salmon fishcakes

INGREDIENTS

500 g (1 lb 4 oz) poached salmon
2 boiled potatoes, finely chopped
3 eggs
1 tsp Dijon mustard
1 tsp sweet mustard
1 tsp mayonnaise
50 g (2 oz) fresh dill, finely
   chopped
50 g (2 oz) fresh parsley, finely
   chopped
50 g (2 oz) fresh chives, finely
   chopped

SERVES 4, COOKING TIME 40 MINUTES

This traditional recipe is given an extra kick with some Dijon mustard and fresh herbs.

Slice the salmon into small pieces. Place the salmon and potatoes in a food processor with 2 eggs, mustard, mayonnaise, dill and parsley. Mix into a thick batter, do not overmix.

Separate the batter into 4 portions and shape into discs. Beat the remaining egg in a small bowl and use to brush both sides of each fishcake.

Heat a little olive oil in a frying pan. Fry the fishcakes for about 3 minutes on each side until golden. Place them on a serving plate, sprinkle with chives and drizzle with a little olive oil.

Good accompaniments are baby spinach, walnuts, thin slices of tomato, some red onion rings, slices of lemon and walnut bread.

salad with smoked salmon and figs

INGREDIENTS

150 g (5 oz) mixed lettuce leaves
300 g (10½ oz) cold-smoked
   salmon or gravlax, thinly sliced
4 fresh figs (you can use dried, but
   fresh figs look nicer), halved
1–2 avocados
10 cherry tomatoes in various
   colours
100 g (3 ½ oz) walnuts
lime, to garnish

DRESSING:
2 limes, juice
1 tbsp liquid honey
1 pinch chilli flakes

SERVES 4, COOKING TIME 30 MINUTES

This is an eye-catching and beautiful salad thanks to all the new types of lettuce that are available now. Try to get a mixture of colours and textures. If you prefer, mango makes a great alternative to the figs. The lime and honey dressing refines the flavour by bringing both tartness and sweetness.

Make the dressing by mixing together the lime juice with the honey and chilli flakes.

Arrange the lettuce on a plate. Separate the salmon into small pieces and distribute them evenly over the plate. Remove the stone from the avocados and cut the flesh into pieces. Arrange the avocado and figs on the plate. Top with the tomatoes and sprinkle with walnuts. Pour the dressing over the salad and decorate with lime.

poached salmon with hollandaise sauce or sauce verte

SERVES 8, COOKING TIME 35 MINUTES, PLUS COOLING TIME

Poached salmon is incredibly tasty and you can use it in so many ways that it's good to poach a lot at once. The fish tastes even better when you've left it in its poaching liquid overnight.

Preheat the oven to 100°C/225°F/gas mark ¼. Mix all the ingredients for the poaching liquid and boil it, covered, for about 10 minutes. Set aside and leave to cool.

Pour the liquid into a large ovenproof dish, add the salmon and cook in the oven for about 20 minutes. Using a meat thermometer can help you to tell when the fish is ready. It is cooked when the temperature reaches 48°C/118°F. Always measure the thickest part of the flesh.

Leave the fish to cool in the liquid. Then carefully remove it and place it on a large serving dish.

Serve with boiled or mashed potatoes, salad with tomatoes, capers, chives, a lot of dill, lemon and hollandaise sauce or sauce verte.

Hollandaise sauce:
Melt the butter in a thick-bottomed saucepan over low heat. Whisk in the flour. Add the stock and water. Bring to the boil, stirring constantly, and keep at boiling point for five minutes. Remove the saucepan from the heat. Mix the egg yolks and cream and whisk this mixture into the saucepan. Simmer the sauce over low heat, whisking the whole time until it thickens. Season with lemon juice, salt and black pepper. Serve the sauce warm or cold.

Sauce verte:
Mix the sour cream, yogurt and mayonnaise with the herbs, spinach and garlic. Season with nutmeg, salt and pepper.

INGREDIENTS

1 kg (2 lb 4 oz) salmon, skin and
  bones removed

POACHING LIQUID:
1½–2 litres (2½–3½ pints) water
1 tbsp salt
2 bay leaves
6 white peppercorns
6 black peppercorns
1 onion, sliced
2 carrots, sliced
1 bunch fresh dill, coarsely chopped
3 tbsp white wine vinegar or 3
  tbsp vinegar essence 12% (with
  vinegar essence the salmon will
  be a bit paler)

HOLLANDAISE SAUCE:
50 g (2 oz) butter
1 tbsp fish stock
300 ml (10½ fl oz) water
2 egg yolks
100 ml (3½ fl oz) cream
juice of 1 lemon
salt and white pepper

SAUCE VERTE:
100 ml (3½ fl oz) sour cream
50 g (2 oz) Greek yogurt
50 g (2 0z) mayonnaise
100 g (3½ oz) fresh herbs, such
  as dill, chives, tarragon, parsley,
  sage, chopped
50 g (2 oz) fresh spinach, finely
  chopped
1 garlic clove, minced
pinch of nutmeg
salt and freshly ground black pepper

salmon soup with seafood

INGREDIENTS

500 g (17½ fl oz) salmon fillet,
  skin removed
1 onion, finely chopped
2 garlic cloves, finely chopped
1 leek, finely chopped
a few saffron strands
1 tbsp butter, for frying
1 tbsp fish stock
200–300 ml (3½–7 fl oz) water
200 ml (7 fl oz) dry white wine
100 ml (3½ fl oz) cream
20 peeled large prawns
10 large cooked mussels in their
  shells
1 bunch fresh coriander

SERVES 4, COOKING TIME 15 MINUTES

Colourful soup with the taste and smell of the sea. Lots of big mussels in their shells and plenty of prawns add to the feeling of indulgence in this dish.

Cut the salmon into 4–6 pieces. Fry the onion, garlic, leek and saffron in butter in a large saucepan or sauté pan. Add the fish stock, water and wine. Simmer uncovered for about 10 minutes. Pour in the cream and carefully add the salmon. Simmer for about 5 more minutes.

Add the prawns and mussels and warm them without cooking them. Cut some coriander and add it on top before serving the soup.

salmon quiche

INGREDIENTS

PASTRY:
150 g (5 oz) flour
150 g (5 oz) butter
3 tbsp water

FILLING:
150 g (5 oz) salmon fillet, skin
  removed
2 spring onions
125 g (4½ oz) prawns
200 ml (7 fl oz) cream
3 eggs
salt and freshly ground black
  pepper

TO GARNISH:
dill or chives
peeled prawns
slices of lime

SERVES 4, COOKING TIME 1 HOUR 30 MINUTES

Rub the butter into the flour and add enough water to form a dough. Roll out the dough and carefully use to line a pie dish. Place it in the refrigerator for 30 minutes.

Preheat the oven to 200°C/400°F/gas mark 6.

Slice the salmon into pieces about 2–3 cm large and the spring onions into pieces about 1 cm long. Put the salmon and onions onto the pie dish along with the prawns.

Whisk the cream and eggs together in a bowl and season with salt and black pepper. Pour into the pie dish on top of the fish and onions.

Bake in the oven for about 25 minutes or until the mixture is firm.

Sprinkle with some dill or chives and decorate with large prawns and slices of lime.

salmon frittata

SERVES 4, COOKING TIME 30 MINUTES

A frittata is a sort of omelette, often with a substantial filling, such as potatoes that have been fried in the pan before you add the egg mixture. You finish off the frittata by frying it on the stove or baking it in the oven. A frittata works as lunch or a midnight snack. If you want to make it taste a little stronger, you can add Dijon mustard to the quark.

Fry the potatoes and onions in the rapeseed oil in a large non-stick frying pan with a lid. Whisk the eggs and mix them with the dill and parsley, salt and pepper. Pour the mixture over the potatoes and onions in the pan and let it firm up slightly. Tilt the pan so the mixture is distributed evenly over the potatoes. Fry on low heat for 5 minutes.

Mix the quark and herbs together. Put spoonfuls of the quark and herb mixture on the frittata and top with the salmon slices. Season with salt and black pepper. Put the lid on the pan and fry for another 2–3 minutes over low heat.

Serve with lettuce, cucumber and more herbs.

INGREDIENTS

400 g (14 oz) boiled potatoes, cubed
2 onions, chopped
2 tbsp rapeseed oil
8 eggs
100 g (3½ oz) dill, finely chopped
1 handful fresh parsley, finely chopped
salt and pepper
200 g (7 oz) quark
100 g (3½ oz) herbs, such as oregano, mint, thyme, lemon balm, coriander, finely chopped
150 g (5½ oz) gravlax in slices
salt and black pepper

salmon bake with clarified butter

INGREDIENTS

butter and bread crumbs for the dish
16 cold boiled potatoes, thinly sliced
1 onion, thinly sliced
600 g (1 lb 5 oz) fresh or smoked
  salmon
100 g (3½ oz) fresh dill, finely chopped
300 ml (10½ fl oz) milk
100 ml (3½ fl oz) cream
2 eggs
2–3 tbsp butter
salt and freshly ground black pepper
dill and lemon slices, to garnish

Tip!

The breadcrumbs in the dish aren't essential, but they make the bake crispier.

SERVES 4, COOKING TIME 45 MINUTES, PLUS CHILLING TIME

A perfect classic dish if you have leftover salmon; fresh, smoked, gravlax, whatever you have will work. Make a double portion as this can last a few days.

Butter an ovenproof dish and sprinkle it with breadcrumbs. Cut the salmon into small pieces. Layer potatoes, onions, salmon and dill in the dish. Season with salt and pepper between the layers but be careful about using too much salt if you are including smoked salmon. Whisk the milk, cream and eggs together. Pour the egg mixture over the fish and vegetables and put the dish in the refrigerator for at least 1 hour.

Preheat the oven to 225°C/435°F/gas mark 7. Dot some butter on top of the chilled mixture and bake for about 25 minutes or until the egg mixture is firm. Turn out onto a plate.

Melt a little butter in a saucepan or the microwave. Decorate the salmon pudding with dill and lemon slices and serve it with the melted butter and mixed lettuce leaves, cherry tomatoes, sugar snap peas, sprouts, spring onions and nuts.

cheesy salmon with crispy cheese biscuit

INGREDIENTS

400 g (14 oz) salmon fillet, skin
  removed, finely chopped
200 g (7 oz) grated cheese, Swedish Västerbotten works well
salt and freshly ground black
  pepper
100 g (3½ oz) fresh dill, chopped,
  to garnish

CRISPY CHEESE BISCUIT:
4 tbsp coarsely grated cheese

Tip!

Watch the biscuits very carefully
as they burn easily. They won't
taste good if they turn too dark.

SERVES 4, COOKING TIME 40 MINUTES

**These salmon balls are very simple to make. The crispy
cheese biscuits are an elegant and indulgent addition.**

Preheat the oven to 150°C/300°F/gas mark 2. Line a baking
tray with greaseproof paper and divide the cheese for the
biscuits into four piles. Bake for about 10 minutes until each
pile has spread out and the biscuits are light brown. Remove
from the oven and leave the biscuits to cool.

Increase the temperature to 180°C/350°F/gas mark 4. Mix
the salmon with the grated cheese and season with salt and
pepper. Shape four balls and place them on a greased baking
tray. Bake in the oven for about 15 minutes.

Place a salmon ball on each plate. Sprinkle with dill and
add a cheese biscuit. Serve with sugar snap peas and cherry
tomatoes.

salmon salad with sardines

SERVES 4, COOKING TIME 15 MINUTES

A beautiful lunch salad with many tasty ingredients that is quick and easy to prepare. I use organic salmon in this dish, which is somewhat lighter in colour.

Arrange the lettuce on a large plate. Rinse the beans in a colander and add them to the lettuce. Make thin strips of cucumber using a potato peeler. Add the cucumber, onion, halved eggs, cherry tomatoes and capers to the salad. Drain the sardines and cut them with scissors into smaller pieces (it's easier than slicing them). Distribute the pieces evenly over the salad. Shape the salmon into small rounds and arrange on top of the salad.

    Garnish with lemon wedges and season with black pepper. Mix the olive oil with the lemon juice and drizzle over the salad.

INGREDIENTS

2 handfuls rocket
2 handfuls lamb's lettuce
1 can kidney beans
1 can large white beans
1 cucumber
1 red onion, thinly sliced
6 hard-boiled eggs, sliced in half
12 yellow cherry tomatoes
10 large capers
1 tin sardine fillets
12 slices gravlax (about 600 g/1 lb 5 oz)
lemon wedges
freshly ground black pepper
50 ml (2 fl oz) olive oil
juice of 2 lemons

creamy salmon pasta salad

INGREDIENTS

500 g (1 lb 2 oz) pasta, such as
    penne
400 g (14 oz) gravlax, in pieces
1 lettuce, shredded
1 apple, cored and sliced
300 ml (10½ fl oz) crème fraîche
100 g (3½ oz) dill, chopped
100 g (3½ oz) chives, chopped
1 tbsp Dijon mustard
salt and freshly ground black
    pepper

SERVES 4, COOKING TIME 30 MINUTES

Pasta is such a versatile ingredient. Cold or warm and in filling salads – you can add just about anything to it. Any leftovers are perfect to take in a lunchbox.

Cook the pasta according to the packet instructions. Rinse under cold water and leave to cool.

Mix together the lettuce, crème fraîche, dill, chives, Dijon mustard and apples in a large bowl. Slice the salmon into cubes about 1½ cm large and add them to the mixture. Mix everything together carefully and stir in the pasta. Season with salt and pepper and garnish with more dill and chives.

hearty salmon salad with bulgur wheat

SERVES 4, COOKING TIME 40 MINUTES

Salanova is a beautiful lettuce with nice dark leaves that has begun to appear in grocery stores. I love trying new types of lettuce and experiencing their unique characters.

Cook the bulgur wheat according to the packet instructions. Set aside and leave to cool. Place the lettuce in a large bowl, add the tomatoes, eggs, sugar snap peas and cooled bulgur wheat. Rinse the kidney beans in cold water and drain them in a colander. Add them to the salad and mix carefully. Cut the salmon into smaller pieces and add to the salad. Sprinkle with herbs and squeeze over the lemon juice. Drizzle with a little olive oil and season with salt and black pepper.

INGREDIENTS

12 thin slices cold-smoked salmon (about 500 g/1 lb 2 oz)
200 g (7 oz) bulgur
1 salanova or other dark-leaved lettuce
1 lettuce of your choice
150 g (5½ oz) tender lettuce, such as baby spinach, rocket, chard
10–15 cherry tomatoes, halved
4 hard-boiled eggs, peeled and halved
150 g (5½ oz) sugar snap peas
1 can kidney beans
100 g (3½ oz) finely chopped fresh herbs, such as oregano, parsley, dill, coriander or thyme
juice of 1 lemon
olive oil
salt and freshly ground black pepper

potato cake with smoked salmon

INGREDIENTS

4–5 potatoes
1 small courgette/zucchini
1 onion
1 egg
about 250 g (9 oz) cold-smoked
  salmon
butter
salt and freshly ground black
  pepper

TO SERVE:
lettuce, spring onions, fresh chives
  and crème fraîche

SERVES 4, COOKING TIME 25 MINUTES

A wonderfully flavourful dish, perfect for lunch or an evening snack. Potato, courgette (zucchini) and onion make the perfect cake for smoked salmon. If you want a stronger flavour, add a little Dijon mustard or horseradish to the crème fraîche.

Peel and coarsely grate the potatoes and courgette (zucchini). Place the grated vegetables on kitchen towels and squeeze out as much moisture as possible before putting in a bowl. Grate the onion and mix it in well. Add the egg and season with salt and pepper.

Melt the butter in a non-stick frying pan and add half the mixture. Smooth it out into a pancake and fry over medium heat for about 8 minutes. Turn the cake over when it seems firm and make sure it is cooked through golden on both sides. Set aside on a plate and make another cake with the rest of the batter. It is easier to make two small cakes than one large one.

Slice the smoked salmon into thin ribbons and place it on top of the cakes. Serve immediately with lettuce, spring onions, chives and a spoonful of crème fraîche.

green pea purée with smoked salmon

SERVES 4, COOKING TIME 20 MINUTES

Yummy peas together with wonderful smoked salmon and horseradish cream. If you want to make it more luxurious, add a glass of sparkling wine just before serving.

Defrost the peas, blend in a food processor then add the cream, stock and water. Mix until the purée is smooth. Pour into a saucepan and warm through – do not let the mixture boil. Squeeze in the lemon juice and season with salt and pepper.

Whip the cream and add the horseradish. Taste it to check the strength and add a little more horseradish if you like.

Cut the salmon into ribbons and divide between four deep plates. Pour the purée around the salmon and add a little horseradish on top.

INGREDIENTS

500 g (1 lb 2 oz) green peas
200 ml (7 fl oz) double cream
1 tbsp vegetable stock
100 ml (3½ fl oz) water (or more, for a looser consistency)
1 tsp lemon juice
300 g (10½ oz) cold-smoked salmon
salt and freshly ground black pepper

HORSERADISH CREAM:
100 ml (3½ fl oz) double cream
1 tbsp grated horseradish

Tip!

The purée can also be served cold.

pasta salad with salmon and pesto

INGREDIENTS

500 g (1 lb 2 oz) cold-smoked
  salmon
500 g (1 lb 2 oz) pasta, such as
  conchiglie
olive oil
2–3 tbsp pesto
1 red onion, finely sliced
10 sun-dried tomatoes, chopped
1 jar artichokes in oil
100 g (3½ oz) sunflower seeds
10–15 asparagus spears
1 garlic clove, minced
Parmesan shavings
salt and freshly ground black
  pepper

SERVES 4, COOKING TIME 40 MINUTES

This tasty salad could hardly be simpler to make. It can be prepared well in advance and is perfect for a picnic outdoors.

Cook the pasta according to the packet instructions until al dente. Rinse in cold water and stir in 1 tbsp olive oil. Put the pasta in a salad bowl and mix with the pesto. Chop the artichokes into smaller pieces and add to the pasta with the onion and sun-dried tomatoes. Season with salt and pepper and mix well.

Roast the sunflower seeds in a hot frying pan. Cut the asparagus into smaller pieces and fry for a few minutes in a little olive oil along with the minced garlic.

Cut the salmon into small cubes and place on top of the pasta. Top with the asparagus and sprinkle over the sunflower seeds and Parmesan.

salmon Thai curry

INGREDIENTS

500 g (1 lb 2 oz) salmon fillet, skin
  removed
1 leek, finely sliced
2 onions, finely chopped
2 garlic cloves, finely chopped
1 red pepper, thinly sliced
butter, for frying
1–2 tbsp green curry paste
100 ml (3½ fl oz) double cream
200 ml (7 fl oz) white wine
1 tbsp fish stock
200 ml (7 fl oz) water
10–15 large prawns, peeled
salt and freshly ground black
  pepper
small bunch of fresh parsley, to
  garnish

SERVES 4, COOKING TIME 30 MINUTES

**This curry smells wonderful and only improves if made
in advance, so all the flavours have time to develop. Be
generous with the prawns and the curry will be even better.**

Fry the onion, leek, garlic and pepper in a little butter in a
large saucepan or sauté pan. Add the curry paste, cream,
wine, stock and water. Simmer, covered, for about 10 minutes.
Season with salt and pepper.

Cut the salmon into four pieces, add to the curry and simmer for about 8 minutes. Add the prawns last; they shouldn't
be boiled. Decorate with large parsley leaves. Serve the stew
with rice or noodles.

warm-smoked salmon with mustard sauce

SERVES 4, COOKING TIME 15 MINUTES, PLUS 1 HOUR CHILLING TIME

This simple and speedy recipe is really easy to make and it's delicious, especially with the sauce and the accompaniments.

Mix all the ingredients for the sauce together and chill in the refrigerator for at least an hour.

Melt a small knob of butter in a frying pan and lightly fry the asparagus. Make sure the asparagus doesn't overcook and remains al dente. Sprinkle with salt.

Place the salmon on a large dish along with the asparagus. Garnish with slices of lemon and serve the sauce in a bowl alongside.

INGREDIENTS

600 g (1 lb 5 oz) warm-smoked
  salmon
2 tbsp butter for frying
asparagus spears
salt
lemon slices, to garnish

MUSTARD SAUCE:
1 tbsp Dijon mustard
1 tbsp sweet mustard
100 ml (3½ fl oz) Greek yogurt
200 ml (7 fl oz) crème fraîche
salt and freshly ground black
  pepper

fried salmon with Cajun spices

INGREDIENTS

4 salmon fillets
300 g (10½ oz) jasmine rice
butter for frying + 50 g (2 oz)
   melted butter
50 g (2 oz) fresh coriander, finely
   chopped
juice of half a lemon

CAJUN SPICES:
1 tsp salt
2 garlic cloves, minced
2 tsp black pepper
1 tsp ground cumin
1 red chilli, chopped
1 tsp paprika
2 tsp barbecue seasoning, or your
   own favourite spice blend

Tip!

Make a double portion of Cajun spice and store it in a jar. It's great sprinkled over chicken or prawns.

SERVES 4, COOKING TIME 30 MINUTES

Salmon can be endlessly adapted. Here a Nordic favourite meets the spices of Louisiana.

Cook the rice according to the packet instructions. Melt a small knob of butter in a frying pan and fry the cooked rice lightly. Add the coriander to the pan and set aside while you prepare the rest of the recipe. Wrap some foil over the pan to keep the rice warm.

Mix all the spices together in a bowl. Roll the salmon pieces in the melted butter and sprinkle with spices on both sides. Fry the salmon in a hot pan for about 2 minutes on each side. Press down on the salmon with a spatula to get a crispy surface. There might be quite a bit of smoke when you do this so put the fan on!

Serve the salmon with the fried rice and squeeze over a little lemon juice to finish.

Main Courses

Easy-to-make and traditional or imaginative and unexpected
flavour combinations – let dinner be the highlight of the day
with fantastic salmon taking centre-stage.

salmon pasta with mushrooms

INGREDIENTS

500 g (1 lb 2 oz) gravlax
500 g (1 lb 2 oz) tagliatelle
600 g (1 lb 5 oz) mushrooms,
  finely sliced
2 tbsp butter for frying
300 ml (10½ fl oz) cream
1 bunch fresh dill, coarsely
  chopped
freshly ground black pepper
100 g (3½ oz) Parmesan, grated

SERVES 6, COOKING TIME 40 MINUTES

This is the simplest pasta dish. Make sure you don't over-cook the salmon, it should be raw in the middle.

Cook the tagliatelle according to the packet instructions.

Fry the mushrooms in butter until they are soft and have browned slightly. Pour in the cream and most of the dill and simmer for a few moments. Slice the salmon into cubes and add it to the pan. Simmer everything for a few minutes.

Pour the sauce over the pasta and add some freshly ground black pepper. Sprinkle with more dill and Parmesan.

Serve with a salad, such as iceberg lettuce with sun-dried tomatoes and toasted pine nuts. Perfect with a glass of Italian red wine.

salmon skewer with bacon

INGREDIENTS

600 g (1 lb 5 oz) salmon fillet, skin
  removed
1 bunch fresh basil
6 bacon rashers
2–3 tbsp olive oil for frying
Parmesan

WARM SALAD:
broccoli
cauliflower
cherry tomatoes
lettuce
fresh basil
salt and freshly ground black
  pepper

SERVES 4, COOKING TIME 30 MINUTES

Salmon is perfect for grilling because it's a fairly oily fish, which means that it absorbs flavours – such as here with the smoked bacon.

Fry the broccoli florets, some cauliflower florets and the cherry tomatoes in a little olive oil for a few minutes. Arrange the lettuce on a large plate. Place the fried vegetables on top and sprinkle over some basil. Season with salt and freshly ground black pepper.

Cut the salmon into large cubes and thread them onto a wooden skewer. Add basil leaves between the salmon cubes. If you use double skewers, the salmon won't spin around. Soaking the skewers in water for a few minutes will stop them from burning. Wrap 1–2 slices of bacon around each skewer.

Light up the grill or barbecue and wait for it to get really hot. The charcoal should be grey if you are using a barbecue.

Grill the skewer for 4–5 minutes on all sides until the bacon is crispy.

Serve with the salad and grate some Parmesan on top.

grilled salmon steaks with chilli béarnaise

SERVES 4, COOKING TIME 1 HOUR

This is a great dish for entertaining. Both the sauce and the ratatouille can be made in advance, leaving you time to talk with your guests.

CHILLI BEARNAISE:
Melt the butter and set aside to cool. Put the water, vinegar, onion and pepper in a small saucepan and boil, uncovered, until the liquid has reduced by half. Strain and pour the liquid back into the saucepan. Half-fill a larger saucepan with water and bring to a simmer. Put the smaller saucepan inside to make a bain-marie. Whisk the egg yolks into the strained liquid. Slowly simmer the sauce, whisking constantly, until the mixture thickens. Remove it from the bain-marie and add the butter a little at a time, stirring all the time. Season with chilli flakes, salt and perhaps some chopped fresh tarragon.

RATAOUILLE:
Heat the olive oil in a large deep-sided frying pan and fry the onion and garlic for a few minutes. Add the other vegetables and fry for a few more minutes until softened. Pour in the tomatoes. Add the oregano, rosemary, black pepper and chilli. Season with salt and perhaps a little sugar.

Cook for about 20 minutes over a low heat, stirring every now and then.

Light the grill and wait for it to get really hot. Brush the salmon steaks with a little olive oil and season them with black pepper. Grill the steaks for 2–3 minutes on each side.

Serve immediately with a spoonful of chilli béarnaise, ratatouille and salad.

INGREDIENTS

4 salmon steaks (about 600 g/
   1 lb 5 oz)
1 tbsp olive oil
salt and freshly ground black
   pepper

CHILLI BEARNAISE:
150 g (5½ oz) butter
3 tbsp water
3 tbsp tarragon vinegar
1 tbsp finely chopped onion
10 black peppercorns, crushed
3 egg yolks
½ tsp chilli flakes
salt
fresh tarragon (optional)

RATATOUILLE:
2 onions, chopped
3 garlic cloves, chopped
1 courgette/zucchini, sliced
1 aubergine/eggplant, sliced
1 green pepper, sliced
1 red pepper, sliced
3 tbsp olive oil
2 tins chopped tomatoes
½ tsp oregano
½ tsp rosemary
½ –1 red chilli, finely chopped
freshly ground black pepper
salt and sugar, to season

Tip!

The salmon in this recipe can be replaced with lamb.

MAIN COURSES

salmon stew with wine

INGREDIENTS

600 g (1 lb 5 oz) salmon fillet, skin
    removed
8 potatoes, peeled
1 onion, chopped
2 spring onions, chopped
butter, for frying
1 garlic clove minced
200 ml (7 fl oz) dry white wine
100 g (3½ oz) mascarpone
50 g (2 oz) finely chopped herbs,
    such as sage, thyme, tarragon,
    parsley or oregano
salt and freshly ground black
    pepper
fresh herbs, to garnish

SERVES 4, COOKING TIME 30 MINUTES

**An everyday stew that gets a boost from fresh herbs. Use
plenty to give extra flavour and colour.**

Boil the potatoes for about 20 minutes until they are soft.
Drain off the water then set aside. Fry all the onions in butter
in a saucepan. Add the minced garlic followed by the wine.
Cut the salmon into pieces, add to the saucepan and simmer
for about 10 minutes.

Carefully take out the salmon pieces and place them on a
warm dish. Mix the mascarpone and chopped herbs into the
saucepan and season with salt and pepper.

Pour the sauce over the salmon and mash the potatoes
with some milk and butter, placing them in a pile beside the
fish.

salmon burger with rice pilaf

SERVES 4, COOKING TIME 30 MINUTES

Sassy burgers are perfect for a weeknight. Try sweet chilli sauce instead of the relish. The rice pilaf makes the dish complete.

Weigh the rice, rinse it in cold water and pour into a saucepan. Add the water, a pinch of salt and the stock cube. Bring to the boil and stir. Cover the saucepan and cook over low heat for about 20 minutes without stirring.

Melt some butter in a frying pan and gently fry the chopped onion. When the rice is almost ready, add the onion and the slightly defrosted peas. Keep the rice in the saucepan with the lid on until the burgers are ready.

Preheat the oven to 125°C/240°F/gas mark 1/2. Coarsely chop the salmon fillet and season with salt and pepper. Shape four burgers using your hands. Heat the rapeseed oil in a frying pan and fry the burgers on both sides for a few minutes. Once they have coloured, place in the oven for about 10 minutes to cook through.

Mix the crème fraîche with the ajvar relish. Taste it to check the spiciness is just right and season with salt and pepper. Add a pinch of sugar if you like.

Place a bed of rice on each plate then put a salmon burger and a large spoonful of ajvar sauce on top. Garnish with fresh red pepper and some lime slices.

INGREDIENTS

about 600 g (1 lb 5 oz) salmon
   fillet, skin removed
salt and freshly ground black
   pepper
1–2 tbsp rapeseed oil

RICE PILAF:
300 g (1½ oz) basmati rice
500 ml (16 fl oz) water
pinch of salt
1 vegetable stock cube
1 onion
1 tbsp butter
200–300 g (7–10½ oz) frozen peas

AJVAR SAUCE:
200–300 ml (7–10½ fl oz) crème
   fraîche
1–2 tbsp ajvar relish (medium)
salt and freshly ground black
   pepper
1–2 tbsp butter, for frying

red pepper and lime, to garnish

salmon on a bed of spinach

INGREDIENTS

8 potatoes
600 g (1 lb 5 oz) salmon fillet, cut
  into 4 portions
500 g (1 lb 2 oz) frozen spinach
1 tbsp butter
½ tsp coarsely grated nutmeg
salt, freshly ground black pepper
  and pink peppercorns
olive oil

Tip!

Choose a fillet from the middle of the salmon so it cooks more evenly.

SERVES 4, COOKING TIME 30 MINUTES

This dish couldn't be easier. If you want to make it a bit more filling, you can add 100 ml (3½ fl oz) double cream and mince some garlic over the fish.

Preheat the oven to 200°C/400°F/gas mark 6. Boil the potatoes for about 20 minutes until they are soft. Drain off the water, put kitchen towels over the saucepan and put the lid on so the potatoes don't go watery.

Defrost the spinach and squeeze out as much liquid as you can. Butter an ovenproof dish. Place the spinach in it and season with nutmeg, salt and pepper. Place the salmon pieces on top of the spinach, brush them with a little olive oil and season with salt and pepper. Bake in the middle of the oven for 15–20 minutes. You can use a meat thermometer to check when the salmon is perfectly cooked. When the inner temperature of the fish reaches 50°C/122°F the salmon is ready.

Mash the potatoes and serve alongside the fish.

grilled gravlax

INGREDIENTS

500–600 g (1 lb 2 oz–1 lb 5 oz)
  gravlax, skin removed
2 aubergines/eggplants
2 small courgettes/zucchinis,
  halved lengthwise
4–5 spring onions, halved lengthwise
4–8 cherry tomatoes, halved
1–2 peppers, sliced
2 garlic cloves, minced
olive oil
salt and freshly ground black
  pepper

SAUCE:
300 ml (10½ fl oz) sour cream
100 g (3½ oz) finely chopped mint
juice of 1–2 limes
½ tsp chilli flakes
1 tbsp runny honey

SERVES 4, COOKING TIME 1 HOUR

Offer something delicious from the barbecue. You can use your grill for this recipe if it's not barbecue weather.

Light the barbecue or grill and let it get really hot.

Slice each aubergine (eggplant) into 4 pieces lengthwise. Mix the garlic with the olive oil, salt and pepper. Brush the garlic oil over all the vegetables and set aside to marinate. Meanwhile mix together the ingredients for the sauce and slice the gravlax.

Place the vegetables on the grill. Keep in mind that some vegetables will take longer than others to cook through, so put the aubergine (eggplant) on first, followed by the courgettes (zucchinis), spring onions and finally the tomatoes. When the vegetables are almost ready, lightly season the fish and grill for a couple of minutes on each side.

Serve the salmon and vegetables along with the prepared sauce.

mustard-crusted salmon with cucumber sauce

SERVES 4, COOKING TIME 30 MINUTES

This is a rather mild dish that could be made hotter by adding Dijon mustard. It uses store cupboard ingredients so is great for a midweek supper.

Start with the sauce. Chop the cucumber and mix it with the crème fraîche. Season with salt and pepper and add the chopped chives. Keep the sauce in the refrigerator while you prepare the salmon.

Preheat the oven to 225°C/435°F/gas mark 7. Grease an ovenproof dish and place the salmon in it. Mix the mustards together and spread the mixture over the salmon. Sprinkle with breadcrumbs.

Bake in the oven for about 20 minutes. You can use a meat thermometer to check when the salmon is cooked. The thickest part of the flesh should measure 50°C/120°F.

Garnish the salmon with lettuce and lemon wedges and serve the sauce in a bowl alongside the fish.

INGREDIENTS

500–600 g (1 lb 2 oz–1 lb 5 oz)
  salmon fillet, skin removed
1 tbsp butter
1–2 tbsp sweet mustard
1–2 tbsp Dijon mustard
50 g (2 oz) breadcrumbs
lettuce and lemon, to garnish

CUCUMBER SAUCE:
1 small cucumber, finely chopped
200 ml (7 fl oz) crème fraîche
salt and freshly ground black
  pepper
2–3 tbsp chopped chives

Russian salmon pierogis

INGREDIENTS

225 g (8 oz) gravlax
2 eggs
500 g (1 lb 4 oz) puff pastry
  sheets, defrosted if frozen
1 onion, finely chopped
2–3 garlic cloves, minced
oil, for frying
200 g (7 oz) fresh spinach
50 g (2 oz) fresh dill, finely
  chopped
50 g (2 oz) fresh chives, finely
  chopped
salt and freshly ground black
  pepper
½ tsp grated nutmeg
egg yolk, to glaze

SERVE WITH:
Lettuce, red onion rings, boiled,
  beetroot, sliced pickled cucumbers, capers, mushrooms,
  roasted onions

SERVES 4, COOKING TIME 1 HOUR 30 MINUTES

This is an old recipe that tastes wonderful with the Russian-inspired accompaniments. A frosty glass of vodka alongside would be an extra treat.

Preheat the oven to 225°C/425°F/gas mark 7. Boil the eggs for 7–8 minutes and set aside to cool. Roll out the pastry sheets to double their size on a floured work surface. Fry the onion and garlic in a little oil until soft, but don't let them brown. Set aside and leave to cool. Fry the spinach.

Distribute the onions, spinach, dill and chives between the rolled out pastry, setting them on one half of each of the pastry sheets. Slice the salmon into small pieces and chop the eggs. Add the salmon and eggs to the pastry. Season with salt, pepper and nutmeg.

Brush around the edges of the pastry with egg yolk and fold the pastry over. If you like you can shape the pastry into a crescent. Press the edges with a fork and brush the all over with egg yolk.

Bake the pierogis in the oven for about 25 minutes. Serve with your choice of accompaniments; sour cream or Russian smetana and sourdough bread are all wonderful.

salmon with sage butter

SERVES 4, COOKING TIME 45 MINUTES

This is not for those who are counting calories, but sometimes you need to just enjoy yourself. Yum!

Preheat the oven to 225°C/425°F/gas mark 7. Grease an oven-proof dish and place the salmon inside. Set a meat thermometer into the thickest part of the fish and place the dish in the oven.

Melt the butter in a small saucepan and add the chopped sage. When the salmon is almost ready and the inner temperature is 48°C/118°F, pour the butter over it. Leave it in the oven for a few more minutes so the salmon absorbs the sage flavour.

Boil the ravioli according to the packet instructions. Be careful to not overcook the pasta. Take the dish from the oven and place the ravioli around the salmon. Season with salt and pepper and grate plenty of Parmesan over the top. Garnish with sage leaves.

INGREDIENTS

500–600 g (1 lb 2 oz–1 lb 5 oz) salmon, skin removed
50 g (2 oz) butter
15 fresh sage leaves, finely chopped
500 g (1 lb 2 oz)fresh ravioli with ricotta filling
salt and freshly ground black pepper
Parmesan
sage leaves, to garnish

stew with salmon and prawns

INGREDIENTS

500–600 g (1 lb 2 oz–1 lb 5 oz)
   salmon fillet, skin removed
2–3 large tomatoes, chopped
butter, for frying
100–200 ml (3½ –7 fl oz) water
1 fish stock cube
200 ml (7 fl oz) cream
1 handful fresh dill, chopped
20–25 peeled prawns
salt and freshly ground black
   pepper

SERVES 4, COOKING TIME 30 MINUTES

As with most stews, this one improves if you leave it over-night. When you're ready to eat, place the prawns on top and warm the stew.

Cut the salmon into cubes. Melt the butter in a frying pan and lightly fry the salmon and tomatoes. Add the water and crumble in the stock cube. Pour the cream in and let everything simmer gently. Stir it carefully so the salmon doesn't break apart.

Add the chopped dill and season with salt and pepper. Finally, put the peeled prawns on top and enjoy this very simple and tasty dish.

Serve with boiled or mashed potatoes.

salmon skewer with spicy sausage

INGREDIENTS

600 g (1 lb 5 oz) salmon fillet, skin
  removed
2 large spicy sausages
8 cherry tomatoes
olive oil
1 garlic clove, minced
1 sprig rosemary, finely chopped
1 sprig thyme, finely chopped

SAFFRON AIOLI:
3 garlic cloves, minced
juice of 1 lime
2 egg yolks
200 ml (7 fl oz) rapeseed oil
pinch of saffron
salt and freshly ground black
  pepper

SERVES 4, COOKING TIME 15 MINUTES

An exciting combination that spreads wonderful scents from the grill, where the smokiness of the sausage flavours the salmon. The saffron aioli is the finishing touch.

Light up the grill and wait for it to get really hot. Soak 4–8 wooden skewers in water for a few minutes to prevent them from burning.

Cut the salmon and sausages into pieces and thread them on the skewers along with the tomatoes. You can use double skewers so the salmon pieces don't roll around.

Grill the skewers for 3–4 minutes on each side. Brush them with a little oil mixed with minced garlic, thyme and rosemary just before they're done.

Serve the skewers with the sauce. Good accompaniments would be a salad, white beans and red onion rings.

SAFFRON AIOLI:
Mix the minced garlic with the lime juice in a bowl. Add the egg yolks. Slowly drizzle the oil into the bowl, stirring the whole time. Mix in the saffron and season with salt and pepper.

oven-baked salmon with pesto

INGREDIENTS

600 g (1 lb 5 oz) salmon, with the
skin left on
5 tbsp pine nuts

PESTO:
75 g (2½ oz) pine nuts
2 bunches fresh basil
200 ml (7 fl oz) good quality olive
oil
2 garlic cloves
100 g (3½ oz) Parmesan, grated
salt and freshly ground black
pepper

SERVE WITH:
Crush boiled potatoes mixed with
olive oil, grated parmesan and
chopped basil

Tip!

You can use readymade or home-
made tapenade instead of pesto.

SERVES 4, COOKING TIME 45 MINUTES

You can of course use readymade pesto for this dish, but it's so easy to make your own and definitely worth the little extra effort. For many salmon recipes, it's easier to use salmon with the skin removed, but here it's better to keep the skin on because it helps to hold the fish together.

Start with the pesto. Roast the pine nuts in a dry frying pan over high heat, along with the pine nuts for the fish, this takes just a couple of minutes. Watch them the whole time and stir them often. Mix the basil in a food processor along with most of the roasted pine nuts, reserving a few. Add the oil and garlic. Add the Parmesan and mix again. Season with salt and black pepper.

Preheat the oven to 200°C/400°F/gas mark 6. Place the salmon skin-side down on a greased ovenproof dish. Make a large slice in the salmon, about 1 cm long and 2 cm deep, and fill it with the pesto. You can let some run over the sides as well. Bake the salmon in the oven for about 15 minutes. Use a meat thermometer and take the fish out when the inner temperature reaches 50°C/122°F. Sprinkle with the reserved pine nuts. Serve with a salad and perhaps some tasty mashed potatoes.

Indian salmon

SERVES 4, COOKING TIME 40 MINUTES

Tandoori spice is a beautiful red spice that will appeal to those who like spicy food. If you prefer milder flavours, you can mix the spice with some yogurt.

Preheat the oven to 200°C/400°F/gas mark 6. Grease an ovenproof dish, place the salmon in it and cover the whole fish with the tandoori spice. Bake the fish in the oven for about 20 minutes. The inner temperature should be about 50°C/122°F, which you can measure with a meat thermometer.

While the fish is cooking, make the sauce. Mix the cucumber, mint, yogurt and garlic together. Season with cumin, salt and pepper.

Remove the salmon from the oven and garnish with some beautiful mint leaves and roasted pumpkin seeds. Serve the salmon and sauce with rice, bulgur or quinoa.

INGREDIENTS

600 g (1 lb 5 oz) salmon fillet
3–4 tbsp tandoori spices, dry or in a paste
mint leaves and pumpkin seeds, to garnish

CUCUMBER AND MINT SAUCE:
½ cucumber, finely cubed
100 g (3½ oz) fresh mint, finely chopped
300 ml (10½ fl oz) natural yogurt
1 garlic clove, minced
1 tsp ground cumin
salt and freshly ground black pepper

Thai salmon in foil

INGREDIENTS

4 salmon fillets, skin removed (600
  g/1 lb 5 oz)
1 courgette/zucchini, thinly sliced
1 onion, thinly sliced
4 garlic cloves, finely chopped
4 large tomatoes, chopped
aluminium foil
4 tbsp lime juice
4 tbsp coconut milk
2 tbsp soya sauce
100 g (3½ oz) fresh coriander,
  coarsely chopped
2 lemongrass stalks
salt and freshly ground black
  pepper

SERVES 4, COOKING TIME 35 MINUTES

A wonderful fragrant Asian dish. Cooking fish in foil keeps in all flavours of the aromatics. If you want to make it look a little fancier, you can sprinkle some shredded coconut over the fish before serving it.

Preheat the oven to 225°C/425°F/gas mark 7. Cut 4 pieces of aluminium foil that are the size of A4 pieces of paper. Evenly divide the courgette (zucchini), onion, garlic, tomatoes and salmon amongst the pieces of foil.

Mix together the lime juice, coconut milk and soya sauce and spoon over the fish. Sprinkle with coriander and place half a stalk of lemongrass in each foil wrapper. Fold the foil tightly into packages and bake in the oven for about 25 minutes.

Unfold them onto plates and remove the lemongrass.

Serve with noodles.

oven-baked salmon with teriyaki sauce

SERVES 4, COOKING TIME 40 MINUTES

A really good sweet-and-sour sauce that suits the saltiness of the salmon. This is extra delicious with the seeds, which provide an extra crunch.

Preheat the oven to 200°C/400°F/gas mark 6. Place the salmon in a greased ovenproof dish and brush with plenty of teriyaki sauce. Bake the salmon for about 20 minutes then top with the seed mixture and cook for a few more minutes.

Serve with rice or noodles and cubed fruit.

INGREDIENTS

600 g (1 lb 5 oz) salmon fillet
200 ml (7 fl oz) teriyaki sauce
100 g (3½ oz) mixed seeds, such
  as sesame, pumpkin and sunflower seeds

SERVE WITH:
rice or noodles and pieces of
papaya, mango, kiwi or melon

Tip!

Add some vitamins in the
form of exotic fruits, which
work well with the sweet-
and-sour sauce.

oven-baked herb salmon

INGREDIENTS

600 g (1 lb 5 oz) salmon fillet
3 tbsp herbs de Provence
100 g (3½ oz) finely chopped fresh
  herbs, such as parsley, dill,
  thyme or tarragon
2 tbsp rapeseed oil

FETA CRÈME:
200 g (7 oz) feta cheese
200 ml (7 fl oz) crème fraîche
salt and freshly ground black
  pepper

SERVES 4, COOKING TIME 30 MINUTES

Aromatic spices and fresh herbs are excellent with salmon. In the summer, I plant herbs in large flower boxes. Sometimes I've used so much that only the stalks are left, but fresh new leaves soon grow again.

Preheat the oven to 200°C/400°F/gas mark 6. Place the salmon in a greased ovenproof dish. Sprinkle with the herbs de Provence and fresh herbs. Drizzle with rapeseed oil.

Bake for about 20 minutes at the bottom of the oven so the fresh herbs don't get burned. The fish is ready when the inner temperature reaches 50°C/122°F, which you can measure with a meat thermometer.

Mash the feta with a fork and mix it in a bowl with the crème fraîche. Season with a little salt and pepper.

Serve the salmon with the feta crème and a salad of lettuce, sugar snap peas, sun-dried tomatoes and walnuts.

crusted salmon in the oven

INGREDIENTS

500–600 g (1 lb 2 oz–1 lb 5 oz)
   salmon fillet
1 tsp salt

WITH GORGONZOLA:
200–250 g (7–9 oz) gorgonzola
100 g (3½ oz) fresh parsley, finely
   chopped
75 g (3 oz) breadcrumbs
freshly ground black pepper

WITH TOMATO BUTTER:
125 g (4½ oz) butter at room
   temperature
3–4 tbsp tomato purée
salt and freshly ground black
   pepper

WITH DILL MAYONNAISE:
200 g (7 oz) fresh dill, finely
   chopped
5–6 tbsp mayonnaise
salt and freshly ground black
   pepper

SERVES 4, COOKING TIME 40 MINUTES

The best thing about salmon is that it goes well with just about any flavour so you are free to experiment and use your imagination. Mix a flavour you like with crème fraîche, mayonnaise or butter and spread it on the fish, then put it in the oven. It couldn't be easier!

Preheat the oven to 225°C/425°F/gas mark 7. Place the salmon in a greased ovenproof dish. Lightly season and spread your favourite sauce on top of the fish. Bake in the oven for about 20 minutes.

WITH GORGONZOLA:
Mash the cheese with a fork and mix it with parsley, breadcrumbs and pepper. Serve it with lightly fried broccoli, onions, carrots and parsnips (see photograph).

WITH TOMATO BUTTER:
Mix the butter and the tomato purée together. Season the mixture with salt and pepper. Serve with rocket, tomatoes, large white beans, sugar snap peas and grated Parmesan cheese.

WITH DILL MAYONNAISE:
Mix the dill and mayonnaise together. Season the mixture with salt and pepper. Serve with herby mashed potatoes, slices of lemon and dill.

salmon and monkfish skewer

SERVES 4, COOKING TIME 40 MINUTES

Luxurious and delicious skewers. The roasted fennel seeds with their liquorice flavour are excellent here. It would be useful to have a large mortar and pestle for the herbs and seeds.

Light the grill and let it get really hot. Soak 4–8 wooden skewers in water for a few minutes to prevent them from burning.

Cut the salmon and monkfish into cubes about 4 cm large and thread the pieces onto the skewers along with the cherry tomatoes. Use double skewers so it's easier to turn them.

Warm 1 tbsp oil in a frying pan and roast the fennel seeds, then crush them in a mortar along with a pinch of salt. Mix them with the lemon juice and the rest of the olive oil. Brush the skewers with the mixture and season with salt and pepper. Grill the skewers for 3 minutes on each side.

Serve with lettuce, red onion rings, slices of tomato, beans, fresh herbs and slices of lemon. A spoonful of aioli also goes well with these skewers.

INGREDIENTS

300 g (10½ oz) salmon fillet, skin removed
300 g (10½ oz) monkfish
16 cherry tomatoes
100 g (3½ oz) fennel seeds
juice of 1 lemon
2 tbsp olive oil, for frying and as a marinade
salt and freshly ground black pepper

risotto with salmon, asparagus and sugar snap peas

INGREDIENTS

400 g (14 oz) cold-smoked salmon
1 litre water
2 tbsp vegetable stock
2–3 shallots, finely chopped
2 tbsp olive oil
400 g (14 oz) arborio rice
150 ml (5 fl oz) white wine
50 g (2 oz) butter
200 g (7 oz) grated parmesan
1 lemon, grated peel
200 g (7 oz) fresh asparagus
100 g (3½ oz) sugar snap peas
1 tbsp oil
grated Parmesan and fresh basil,
  to garnish
salt and freshly ground black
  pepper

SERVES 4, COOKING TIME 40 MINUTES

Forget any dry, stodgy risottos you may have eaten in the past – this tasty Italian dish should be runny and utterly delicious. You can flavour it with whatever you have on hand; here I have used asparagus and sugar snap peas both for their taste and their crispy consistency.

Boil the water and stock in a saucepan. Fry the shallots in oil in a different saucepan. Add the rice and fry it for a couple of minutes, then add half the wine. Simmer it over low heat and add the stock a little bit at a time. Add the rest of the wine and cook for another 15 minutes while stirring. The consistency should be a bit like porridge.

Add the butter and Parmesan. Stir well. Season with the lemon peel, salt and pepper.

Cut the asparagus into small pieces. Fry the asparagus and sugar snap peas in a little rapeseed or olive oil and carefully add them to the risotto.

Place the salmon on a serving dish and season with freshly ground black pepper. Top with some Parmesan and basil leaves. Serve the risotto in a bowl alongside the salmon.

fried salmon with chanterelles

INGREDIENTS

POTATO AND CELERIAC PURÉE
½ kg (1 lb 2 oz) potatoes, finely
   sliced
200 g (7 oz) celeriac, finely sliced
100 ml (3½ fl oz) single cream
2 tbsp butter
salt and freshly ground black
   pepper

4 salmon fillets (about 600 g/1 lb
   5 oz)
200 g (7 oz) golden chanterelles, or
   100 g (3½ oz) golden chanterelles and 100 g (3½ oz) funnel
   chanterelles
1–2 onions, finely chopped
2–3 tbsp butter
100 g (3½ oz) smoked ham, cubed
salt

SERVES 4, COOKING TIME 45 MINUTES

Treasures from the forest, earth and sea in a successful union. The golden chanterelles light up the dish so be generous with them. The smoked ham and the purée add lively additional flavours.

Start with the purée: Boil the potatoes and celeriac until soft, about 15 minutes. Meanwhile warm the cream and stir in the butter. Mash the potatoes and celeriac and add the cream and butter. Season with salt and pepper. Cover the purée, set aside and keep warm.

Brush the chanterelles clean and cut the larger ones. Melt the butter in a large frying pan and fry the chanterelles and onions together. Salt lightly. Make sure the mushrooms are browned, soft and thoroughly cooked.

Add the ham for a few minutes at the end. Set the ham and mushrooms aside and fry the salmon over medium heat for 2–3 minutes on each side.

Place the salmon on a serving dish and cover it with mushrooms, onions and ham. Add some potato and celeriac purée. Serve with some lettuce and a flavourful bread.

salmon with pomegranate

INGREDIENTS

500 g (1 lb 4 oz) salmon fillet
300 g (10½ oz) broccoli florets
300 g (10½ oz) chard
3 garlic cloves, crushed
½ tsp nutmeg
300 ml (10½ fl oz) single cream
1 pomegranate
salt and pepper

SERVES 4. COOKING TIME 40 MINUTES

Salmon practically demands sour accompaniments, lemon and lime being the most common. Here the sourness comes from beautiful pomegranate seeds.

Preheat the oven to 220°C/425°F/gas mark 7. Grease an oven-proof dish. Place the broccoli and chard in the dish and scatter over the crushed garlic. Season with salt, pepper and nutmeg. Pour the cream over everything and place the salmon on top. Put the dish in the oven for about 20 minutes, by which time the salmon should be cooked and the vegetables soft. Halve the pomegranate, remove the seeds and sprinkle them over the salmon.

Serve with lettuce, sliced cucumber and pieces of avocado.

salmon in foil with potato, spring onions and sage

SERVES 4, COOKING TIME 40 MINUTES

All the good flavours are retained by the foil package here and the fish is given plenty of time to absorb them.

Light the grill and let it get really hot. Boil the new potatoes until they are soft. Cut the salmon into 8 smaller pieces.

Cut 4 large pieces of aluminium foil. Divide the salmon, potatoes, onions and sage between each piece. Top with butter and season with salt and pepper. Fold the packages together and place them under the grill for about 15 minutes.

Open the packages before serving and top with some fresh sage leaves.

INGREDIENTS

600 g (1 lb 5 oz) salmon fillet, skin removed
½ kg (1 lb 2 oz) new potatoes, halved
1 onion, sliced
4 spring onions, finely sliced
100 g (3½ oz) fresh sage, finely chopped
100 g (3½ oz) butter
sage leaves, to garnish

Tip!

The sage can be replaced with other herbs, such as thyme, tarragon or oregano.

salmon hash

INGREDIENTS

600 g (1 lb 5 oz) salmon fillet
6 potatoes, cubed
1 parsnip, cubed
2 carrots, cubed
1 courgette/zucchini, cubed
2 red onions, chopped
1 bunch fresh dill, finely chopped
1 bunch fresh dill, finely chopped
4 eggs
butter, for frying

SERVES 4, COOKING TIME 15 MINUTES

Super as an evening snack or light meal. Serve with ice-cold beer and some good freshly baked bread.

Fry the vegetables together in a little butter for 6–7 minutes until they are soft but with a slightly crispy surface. Start with the potatoes, which need a little extra time.

Cut the salmon into cubes about 2 x 2 cm and fry for a few minutes in a separate frying pan. Carefully add the salmon to the vegetables. Sprinkle with the dill and parsley.

Fry 4 eggs over medium heat, making sure the yolks stay whole. Serve the eggs on top of the hash.

Index

Atlantic salmon 6

basic recipes 10-11

blinis with salmon and caviar 30

canapés with salmon and caviar 42

char 8

cheesy salmon with crispy cheese biscuit 80

chilli béarnaise 107

chum salmon 6

cold-smoked salmon 10

cooking time 11

creamy salmon pasta salad 84

crusted salmon 136

cured salmon 10

cured salmon with grapefruit 19

English fish cake 66

farmed salmon 6, 8

fat content 8

filling salmon salad with bulgur 87

fishcake 66

gravlax sauce 14

gravlax, grilled 114

green pea puree with smoked salmon 91

grilled gravlax 114

grilled salmon steaks with chilli béarnaise 107

herb salmon, oven-baked 134

hollandaise sauce 71

Indian salmon 129

mustard-breaded salmon with cucumber sauce 116

omega-3 fats 8

open-faced sandwich with poached salmon 38

organic salmon 6

oven-baked herb salmon 134

oven-baked salmon with pesto 126

oven-baked salmon with teriyaki sauce 133

Pacific salmon 6

parasites 9

pasta salad with salmon and pesto 92

pink salmon 6

poached salmon with hollandaise sauce or sauce
    verte 71

potato cake with smoked salmon 88

rainbow trout 9

ratatouille 107

risotto with salmon, asparagus and sugar snap
    peas 140

Russian salmon pierogies 118

salad with smoked salmon and figs 68

Salmo Salar 6

salmon balls with dill 52

salmon bruschetta 23

salmon burger with rice pilaf 111

salmon carpaccio with dill oil 58

salmon ceviche 54

salmon cups with feta and avocado crème 29

salmon fried with Cajun spices 98

salmon fried with chanterelles 142

salmon frittata 77

salmon hash 148

salmon hors d'oeuvre 33

salmon in foil 11

salmon on a bed of spinach 112

salmon parcels with melon and mussels 51

salmon pasta with mushrooms 102

salmon pâté with sardine sauce 44

salmon pie 74

salmon pierogies, Russian 118

salmon pinwheels 41

salmon pudding with clarified butter 78

salmon rolls with cream cheese and wasabi 24

salmon rolls with prawn filling 48

salmon salad with dill and lime 36

salmon salad with fruit and mozzarella 62

salmon salad with new potatoes 65

salmon salad with sardines 83

salmon salsa with coriander 26

salmon skewer with bacon 104

salmon skewer with parsley and melon 34

salmon skewer with spicy sausage 124

salmon soup with seafood 72

salmon steaks, grilled with chilli béarnaise 107

salmon stew with curry 94

salmon stew with wine 108

salmon tartare 16

salmon with pomegranate 144

salmon with sage butter 121

salmon wraps 61

sardine sauce 44

sauce verte 71

skewer with salmon and monkfish 149

smoked salmon with chèvre pesto 47

stew with salmon and prawns 122

storage and freshness 9

sushi with salmon and lemon 20

temperatures 11

Thai salmon in foil 130

to fry salmon 11

to pickle salmon 10

to poach salmon in a saucepan 11

to poach salmon in the oven 10

toasted open-faced salmon sandwich with gravlax
    sauce 14

trout 8

warm-smoked salmon 10

warm-smoked salmon with mustard sauce 97

wild salmon 6

Thank you to Helena Barrsjö-Lundin, Åkersberga, for the beautiful dishes, and to Gamla Stans for the fish

Published by New Holland Publishers 2012
First published by Norstedts, Sweden, in 2011 as Lax Från Vargad Till Lyx

Garfield House 86–88 Edgware Road London W2 2EA United Kingdom
Wembly Square, First Floor Solan Street Gardens Cape Town 8000 South Africa
Unit 1/66 Gibbes Street Chatswood, NSW 2067 Australia
218 Lake Road Northcote, Auckland New Zealand

Text copyright © 2011 Paula Ahlsén Söder
Copyright © 2012 New Holland Publishers
Published by agreement with Norstedts Agency

Editor: Anna Sjögren
Design: Pernilla Qvist
Cover: Celeste Vlok, Photograph: Susanne Hallman
Photographs: Susanne Hallman
Translation: B.J. Epstein
Printer: Toppan Leefung Printing Ltd (China)

ISBN 978 1 78009 151 8

Follow New Holland Publishers on
Facebook: www.facebook.com/NewHollandPublishers